Ravaged and Reborn

Ravaged and Reborn: The Iranian Army, 1982

A Staff Paper by William F. Hickman

THE BROOKINGS INSTITUTION
Washington, D.C.

THE BROOKINGS INSTITUTION is an independent organization devoted to nonpartisan research, education, and publication in economics, government, foreign policy, and the social sciences generally. Its principal purposes are to aid in the development of sound public policies and to promote public understanding of issues of national importance.

The Institution was founded on December 8, 1927, to merge the activities of the Institute for Government Research, founded in 1916, the Institute of Economics, founded in 1922, and the Robert Brookings Graduate School of Economics and Government, founded in 1924.

The Board of Trustees is responsible for the general administration of the Institution, while the immediate direction of the policies, program, and staff is vested in the President, assisted by an advisory committee of the officers and staff. The by-laws of the Institution state: "It is the function of the Trustees to make possible the conduct of scientific research, and publication, under the most favorable conditions, and to safeguard the independence of the research staff in the pursuit of their studies and in the publication of the results of such studies. It is not a part of their function to determine, control, or influence the conduct of particular investigations or the conclusions reached."

The President bears final responsibility for the decision to publish a manuscript as a Brookings book. In reaching his judgment on the competence, accuracy, and objectivity of each study, the President is advised by the director of the appropriate research program and weighs the views of a panel of expert outside readers who report to him in confidence on the quality of the work. Publication of a work signifies that it is deemed a competent treatment worthy of public consideration but does not imply endorsement of conclusions or recommendations.

The Institution maintains its position of neutrality on issues of public policy in order to safeguard the intellectual freedom of the staff. Hence interpretations or conclusions in Brookings publications should be understood to be solely those of the authors and should not be attributed to the Institution, to its trustees, officers, or other staff members, or to the organizations that support its research.

Foreword

AFTER the fall of Shah Muhammed Reza Pahlavi in January 1979, there was much speculation in the West regarding the future of the Iranian military. Its ineffectiveness and rapid collapse during the Islamic revolution came as a shock to those who had believed it to be a strong, dedicated force capable of controlling any domestic unrest. The speculation was driven by reports of numerous executions of high-ranking military officers, mass desertions, and demands by various Iranian groups for the complete dissolution of the military. What arose was a common Western perception of a decimated military establishment that had been replaced by a paramilitary organization composed of fanatical followers of Ayatollah Khomeini, the Revolutionary Guards.

In this staff paper Lieutenant Commander William F. Hickman, U.S. Navy, a 1981–82 federal executive fellow in the Brookings Foreign Policy Studies program, analyzes the statements and actions of the leaders of the Islamic Republic of Iran and outlines the changes imposed upon the military. He maintains that the Islamic government showed a continuity of purpose not generally ascribed to it; that the intent was not to dissolve the military, but rather to recast it in an Islamic mold; that the effort has been successful; and that the Iranian military has been reborn as an effective, as well as Islamic, fighting force.

This paper benefited greatly from the advice and comments of James A. Bill, Gary Sick, Michael K. MccGwire, Thomas L. McNaugher, William Olsen, and Steven Grumman. The author is also grateful to John D. Steinbruner, director of the Brookings Foreign Policy Studies program, who provided valuable guidance; to Elizabeth H. Cross, who edited the manuscript; to Alan G. Hoden, who verified its factual content; and to

Mary Buena, who processed it. The study was partially supported by a grant from the Ford Foundation.

The views expressed herein are those of the author and should not be construed as official positions of either the Department of the Navy or the Department of Defense. Nor should they be ascribed to the Ford Foundation, to those who commented on the study, or to the trustees, officers, or staff members of the Brookings Institution.

BRUCE K. MACLAURY
President

November 1982
Washington, D.C.

Ravaged and Reborn: The Iranian Army, 1982

IN THE WAKE of the Iranian revolution of 1978–79, it became almost a cliché to refer to the decimation of the Iranian army. One cause of this decimation was the wholesale desertion of personnel who were fearful of reprisal, ashamed of their role in the revolution, or otherwise disillusioned with the shah's military. The International Institute for Strategic Studies estimated that by July 1979, 60 percent of the army (about 171,000 men) had deserted.[1] Another cause was the institution by the victorious revolutionaries of a wide and prolonged purge of the armed forces intended to neutralize their counterrevolutionary potential. By the fall of 1980 this had resulted in the dismissal, arrest, trial, imprisonment, or execution of some 10,000 military personnel.[2] Not only were Western-trained officers eliminated, but also revolutionary committees were established at each level of command, Shiite clergy were installed at each base in a role similar to that of political officers in communist regimes, and the breakdown of military discipline was encouraged.

Perhaps the most effective means of neutralizing the armed forces was the establishment of a separate paramilitary force loyal to the regime. Although they lacked formal military training, the Islamic Revolutionary Guards were fanatically loyal, both to Ayatollah Khomeini and to the revolution, and they progressively assumed duties that had been the prerogative of the armed forces. This process was hastened by the periodic discovery during 1980 of military groups plotting the overthrow of the regime.

1. International Institute for Strategic Studies, *The Military Balance, 1979–1980* (London: IISS, 1979), p. 39.
2. Foreign Broadcast Information Service, *Daily Report: South Asia*, October 15, 1980, p. I12.

The September 1980 invasion by Iraq gave the military an opportunity to restore its lost stature and influence in the country, and, despite its lack of success, during the initial months the army did regain its prestige. How much real influence it gained, however, is open to question. After a year of desultory fighting, Iranian forces seized the initiative in late 1981 and by the summer of 1982 had driven the Iraqis out of Iran, seizing a small wedge of Iraqi territory in the process. Does this dramatic improvement on the battlefield reflect a reconstituted Iranian military, the fervor of the Revolutionary Guards, or a combination of the two? Does battlefield success presage a return to prominence for the military in domestic Iranian politics? If not, once the war is concluded what role can the military be expected to play in Iran?

The task of evaluating the effectiveness of a military organization in the Middle East is complicated by the abundance of arms, the diverse threats presented to ruling governments, and the conflicting loyalties that permeate the area. The relevant factors for such an assessment include the military situation facing the country, the size of the armed forces, their organization, their weapons and military equipment, the state of training, the degree of popular support for the military, and less tangible dimensions such as discipline, efficiency, motivation, and morale. And in the case of the Islamic Iranian military, two more qualities are significant: Islamic fervor and Iranian nationalism.

The Imperial Military

When Shah Muhammed Reza Pahlavi flew into exile on January 16, 1979, the military he left behind was a far cry from the one in which he had invested so heavily during his reign. The shah may have hoped that the military would somehow be able to restore him to his throne, but the Imperial Iranian Military was unable to preserve itself, let alone save the monarchy. The armed forces were simply not capable of dealing with the situation they faced as the revolution developed, largely because they were then trained and organized for a very different role.

Both Shah Muhammed Reza and his father, Reza Shah, had used the army to control rebellious tribes throughout Iran and to put down domestic unrest, but after 1963, when the shah used the army to put down street demonstrations in opposition to his "white" revolution, internal security was relegated to a secondary role for the armed forces.[3] Confident that military force could easily handle any internal disturbances that might arise, the shah directed the development and expansion of an outward-looking military that reflected his perception of Iran's strategic position.

The shah believed that the Soviet Union and Iraq were the greatest threats to his country. Lesser threats were seen as insurgency in Oman, separatism among some tribes in Iran, and terrorism throughout the region. This assessment was supported by a 1976 congressional study of U.S. military sales to Iran, which concluded (among other things) that "the military threats to Iran's security seem to be sufficiently real and diverse to enable the Shah to justify major investments in military forces."[4] The military organization that resulted from these perceptions was primarily designed for external rather than domestic requirements.

This outward orientation meant that weapons and training for domestic disturbances were not emphasized. Without these essential weapons and the necessary training, when the military was ordered to break up the mass revolutionary demonstrations, it responded with disproportionate force. The casualties sustained from the lethal weapons employed fueled the crisis by providing martyrs and touched off a cycle of increasing violence and repression.[5]

A major consequence of the shah's redirection was that the military lost whatever capability for effective internal security it had possessed. The shah did not recognize this loss, however, and continued to count on the military as the ultimate guarantor of his reign. During the revolution, when he expected the military to assume a major role in the rapidly deteriorating domestic situation, it was incapable of doing so. Beyond this, however,

3. Responsibility for internal security, including intelligence operations, was relegated to the Imperial Iranian Gendarmerie and SAVAK. Fred Halliday, *Iran: Dictatorship and Development* (Penguin Books, 1979), pp. 76–77. For information relating to the 1963 incident, see Roy Parviz Mottahedeh, "Iran's Foreign Devils," *Foreign Affairs*, no. 38 (Spring 1980), pp. 25–26.

4. *U.S. Military Sales to Iran*, Committee Print, Staff Report to the Subcommittee on Foreign Assistance of the Senate Committee on Foreign Relations, 94 Cong. 2 sess. (Government Printing Office, 1976), p. 12.

5. Several studies of the revolution have noted that the military was ill prepared to handle the level of domestic violence it faced in 1978. See, for example, Robert Graham, *Iran: The Illusion of Power* (St. Martin's, 1979), pp. 232–33; Nikki R. Keddie, *Roots of Revolution: An Interpretive History of Modern Iran* (Yale University Press, 1981), p. 256; and Barry Rubin, *Paved With Good Intentions: The American Experience and Iran* (New York: Oxford University Press, 1980), pp. 225–26.

there were fundamental problems that prevented the military leadership from controlling the situation.

Because a number of military officers had been involved in the 1953 effort to force him from the throne, the shah made a strong effort to ensure the loyalty of the officer corps. Over the next twenty-seven years, he co-opted his officers by purchasing the best military equipment available and by giving them special prerogatives. Admission to the officer corps guaranteed high pay, special importation privileges, access to new housing in a housing-poor country, servants, vacation quarters, and special discount stores. In short, military officers became a new privileged class, wholly dependent on the shah for their livelihood.[6] By providing these benefits, the shah successfully isolated the officer corps from domestic politics and made it completely loyal and subservient to him. The long-term result of this life of privilege and isolation was that the upper ranks of the officer corps lost touch with the Iranian people. Therefore, when the revolution occurred and the shah expected the military to put down the opposition, these officers were unable even to assess the opposition accurately. The junior officers were generally less isolated and much more aware of the currents of opposition, but they could not have provided such an assessment, either. To further complicate the situation, there was no unanimity among the senior officers on the appropriate course of action. A small group argued for harsh measures but was consistently overruled by the shah, who wished to avoid bloodshed.[7]

A more serious problem for the military, however, emanated from the very structure of the armed forces. In theory, each service was headed by a general officer who was a member of the supreme commander's staff, the function of which was to operate as a planning and control center for the shah. This much is similar to the American military system, after which the Iranian military was patterned. In contrast to the American system, however, the commanding generals had little real authority over their commands. As the head of state, the shah was the commander-in-chief of the armed forces, and each of the service chiefs reported to him on a regular basis on all matters concerning the funding, organization, and military direction of his own service. What made this seemingly normal reporting requirement unusual was that the shah made decisions on all kinds of

6. J. C. Hurewitz, *Middle East Politics: The Military Dimension* (Praeger, 1969), p. 286; and Rubin, *Paved With Good Intentions*, pp. 225–26.

7. Former senior general, Imperial Iranian Air Force, interview with author, June 18, 1982; and William H. Sullivan, *Mission to Iran* (Norton, 1981), p. 74.

military activity, not just major policy issues. This made him the de facto commander of the individual services as well,[8] and left little room for the development of initiative. In fact, initiative was the one factor likely to get a senior officer into serious trouble with the shah. Ever conscious of the possibility of a military coup against him, the shah constantly manipulated his senior officers, just as he did other politically influential members of Iranian society. If a senior officer attained a position from which he might derive too much power or influence, he was subject to rapid retirement, demotion, or transfer.[9]

The result of such a system was to promote only officers who would not be a threat to the shah. These officers were astute and loyal and used to receiving detailed instructions on major matters. The system worked quite well until the shah was confronted with a revolution, a situation he could neither understand nor control. Consequently, he could provide no effective guidance to the men he ultimately expected to rescue him from the deteriorating situation. A telling comment on his capabilities during this period was made by General Gholam Reza Azhari, the prime minister of the military government installed by the shah in late 1978. After the shah had prevented the troops from firing on the rioters and demonstrators in an attempt to restore order by force, the general told the U.S. ambassador, "You must know this and you must tell it to your government. This country is lost because the king cannot make up his mind."[10]

Fundamental though the military leadership's problems were, it is doubtful whether, by themselves, they were sufficient to prevent the military from intervening effectively against the demonstrators. Far more important was what was happening to those on the front lines (in the streets).

Quite separate from the loyal cadre of officers who owed their privileged existence to the shah were two other distinct classes: the warrant and noncommissioned officers and the conscripts. The former were drawn largely from the urban middle class,[11] but their attitudes toward the shah were

8. Sullivan, *Mission to Iran*, p. 74.

9. The shah's pattern was well established. In three separate instances, chiefs of the supreme commander's staff were removed without warning. In 1966 General Hijazi, who had been in the position for a number of years, was retired without notice. In 1969 his replacement, General Bahran Ariyana, was similarly retired. Two years later General Firaydun Jam was suddenly removed and appointed ambassador to Spain, an action that was tantamount to political exile. Marvin Zonis, *The Political Elite of Iran* (Princeton University Press, 1971), pp. 22–23; and James Alban Bill, *The Politics of Iran: Groups, Classes, and Modernization* (Merrill, 1972), pp. 42–44.

10. Sullivan, *Mission to Iran*, p. 212.

11. Major John M. Smith, "Where Was the Shah's Army?" (thesis, U.S. Army Com-

different. The NCOs who had risen from the ranks were, in the main, ardent supporters of the shah. Because they could be trusted, during the revolution they were called upon for the dirty work of quelling the domestic unrest. The warrant officers, however, were mainly anti-shah. They were highly trained specialists who filled a variety of technical positions, but while they had received their education from the government, they had not been granted privileges commensurate to those enjoyed by the officer corps. Whether such privileges could have guaranteed their loyalty when they faced a revolution can never be ascertained. What is certain, however, is that as the inevitable crisis over support of the shah occurred within the military, this class formed a strong anti-shah faction.[12]

Even more loosely tied to the shah's regime were the conscripts. At the age of nineteen, all Iranian males were required to register for military service. About half of these would be called up at the age of twenty-one, to serve two years on active duty. Mostly illiterate and drawn from the lower classes of Iranian society, especially the rural areas, these recruits would be subjected to an American-style training program, which included basic training, literacy training, and advanced technical training if they qualified. Because they had not volunteered for duty, however, the conscripts, no matter how much training they received, were never fully trusted by the military cadre. This disparity was reinforced by the imposition of a rigid disciplinary structure on the military caste system, which often kept the conscript in a position of near-servitude. Those who could not qualify for the advanced training were required to perform menial tasks for their superiors, such as gardening and janitorial services or other nonmilitary positions in the households of senior officers. Although the conscript began each day in a military formation, reciting a ritualistic pledge to support God, shah, and country, there was little to make him loyal to the central theme of the ritual, the shah.

For the average conscript, the entire military experience could be bewildering. His simple background had not prepared him for the strange and

---

mand and General Staff College, 1980), pp. 72–77. Major Smith served in Tehran as the foreign military sales training officer in the U.S. Army Mission and Military Assistance Advisory Group to Iran from 1977 to 1979.

12. On the night of February 9 air force warrant officers (*homafars*) joined with a group of air force cadets in rebellion against the air force command. For this and other actions earlier in the revolution, the homafars were regarded as the vanguard of the revolution for several months after the fall of the shah. While most of the military were attempting to keep a low profile during this period, the homafars kept up a visible public presence. As examples, see FBIS, *Daily Report: Middle East*, March 19, 1979, p. R10; and May 29, 1979, p. R12.

hostile environment in which he found himself, separated from his traditional support group of family and friends, and posted to a garrison in a part of Iran where he knew no one, in what appears to have been a calculated effort by the regime to reduce the possibility of his disaffection. Although internal security was only a secondary role for the military, the theory seems to have been that in the event of a threat to the regime from some domestic source, the conscript was more likely to shoot a stranger if necessary than to oppose his friends and relatives. For example, in August 1978 soldiers enforcing martial law in Esfahan were accused by the local residents of being "Baluchi butchers" who would kill a person for eight tumans (a little more than one dollar).[13]

In practice, this plan backfired. Separated from their normal emotional support, the conscripts, who by and large came from fairly religious backgrounds, turned to the only familiar source of comfort still available to them, the mosque. It was from the mosques that the teachings of Ayatollah Khomeini and other anti-shah clerics were being disseminated. The result was that when the conscripts were ordered into the streets to face down the revolutionaries, they were met by people from the same strata of society who held the same values and beliefs as they did, and they confronted a classic moral dilemma. Khomeini had issued special instructions to his followers: "Do not attack the army in its breast, but in its heart." "You must appeal to the soldiers' hearts even if they fire on you and kill you. Let them kill five thousand, ten thousand, twenty thousand—they are our brothers and we will welcome them. We will prove that blood is more powerful than the sword."[14] When demonstrators presented them with flowers and invited them to join in opposing a shah who did not value their religion, many of the conscripts changed sides. For much of 1978 the shah may have believed that he had the support of the military, but in fact that support was fragile and much of it was easily subverted.

The picture that emerges of the Imperial Iranian Military in 1979 is one of an institution in turmoil. Organized for the wrong war, divided by class and loyalty, it could not suppress the opposition, or even estimate its strength, until it was too late. The military was not, however, just a house of cards that collapsed with a slight push. Had the problem in 1979 been a foreign invasion rather than a revolution, it would probably have responded well. But faced with revolutionary fervor, the Imperial Military was hamstrung by its fundamental flaws.

13. American traveler in Iran, 1978, interview with author, May 10, 1982.
14. Mohamed Heikal, *Iran: The Untold Story* (Pantheon Books, 1981), pp. 145–46.

The Purge

"The purging of the armed organizations affiliated with the former diabolical regime is among the top priorities of the new government. It has top priority in the Revolution committee appointed by the Imam Khomeini."[15] That announcement by Ayatollah Khomeini's propaganda committee set the tone for a concentrated effort by the victorious revolutionaries to consolidate their victory by eliminating the most likely source of counterrevolution. What happened over the next few months has been likened by the Western press to the Reign of Terror that followed the French Revolution in 1793, but this is an exaggeration.[16] Although several dozen military officers were executed, it is now known that the purge of the military was much less severe in the early months of Islamic Iran than was originally thought. It was not until much later that the purge cut deeply into the military, and then it affected the army much more than the other services.

Action against the military can be broken down into two distinct periods. The first, a purge limited to senior officers, extended roughly from the establishment of the provisional Islamic government in mid-February 1979 to the appointment of the first civilian minister of national defense in late September of that year. During this period command of the military was entrusted to a group of former military officers who had established their revolutionary credentials by running afoul of the shah before the revolution. The first two ministers of national defense, Rear Admiral Ahmad Madani and General Taqi Riyahi, were the major figures in this group. Under their leadership, efforts were made to stabilize and reorganize the military along Islamic lines.[17] The prevailing theory seemed to be that

15. FBIS, *Daily Report: Middle East and Africa*, February 21, 1979, p. 2. (Hereafter FBIS, *Daily Report: MEA.*)

16. "The Reign of Terror," *Time*, April 23, 1979, p. 32.

17. In addition to Madani and Riyahi, this group included the officers who were selected as the initial chiefs of staff of the armed services, including Major General Mohammed Vali Gharavi, the first chief of staff of the army; Major General Vali Ullah Qarani, his successor; Brigadier General Afsar Imanian, chief of staff of the air force; and Major General Naser Farbod, the third chief of staff of the army. See FBIS, *Daily Report: MEA*, February 21, 1979, pp. R2, R21; February 25, 1979, p. R1; February 13, 1979, p. R3; March 2, 1979, p. R1; and March 30, 1979, p. R4. For examples of statements by these officers on the reorganization of the military, see ibid., March 7, 1979, p. R6; April 3, 1979, p. R5; May 11, 1979, p. R2; May 29, 1979, p. R11; and June 5, 1979, p. R4.

control of the armed forces should rest with experienced military men rather than with dedicated revolutionaries.

Executions during this period were generally limited to the most senior personnel in each service and those who had committed specific counterrevolutionary acts, such as leading or participating in the assaults by the military or the national police against the mass demonstrations. The rest of the purge consisted of the forced retirement, rather than execution, of hundreds of military personnel, including all major generals and most brigadier generals. Retirements of enlisted cadre were mostly from the Imperial Guard, which had been charged with protecting the shah and had most actively opposed the revolution.[18] Surprisingly, these personnel were not summarily dismissed from the services but were actually retired under the provisions of a law enacted during the shah's regime.[19] The executions began on February 15, when the former head of SAVAK, the military governors of Tehran and Esfahan, and the commander of the air force were tried by a revolutionary court and quickly executed for "torture, killing the people, treason and spreading sedition on earth."[20] Despite this bloody beginning, an examination of the announced executions through September indicates that the military was not the primary target of the purge. While it is certain that not all executions were either announced or reported, the figures provide a reasonable estimate of the trends.

Although over 80 percent of the first 200 executed were members of the shah's military and security apparatus, it must be remembered that this figure includes former members of SAVAK and the national police, both of which had been charged with primary responsibility for internal security, making them more likely targets than the military for "revolutionary justice." Of the 404 announced executions over the entire period of the first purge, only 21 percent (85) were of military personnel. In contrast, 37.9 percent (153) were members of SAVAK and the national police. Out of an estimated population of over 200 general officers in the military, 26 were executed and the rest forcibly retired, a further indication that the desire for revolutionary vengeance against the military per se was less strong than previously suspected. Although lower-ranking officers were among those

18. Interview with Major General Vali Qarani in ibid., February 21, 1979, p. R22.
19. Ibid., March 7, 1979, p. R1, gives a partial listing of officers retired under this 1965 law.
20. Ibid., February 16, 1979, p. R10.

executed and retired, there is little evidence of a policy aimed at their wholesale removal, as in the case of the general officers.[21]

As the purge progressed, there were many calls for the dissolution of the armed forces. The three major leftist groups, the Tudeh party (Marxist), the Feda'iyin-e Khalq (a Marxist-Leninist group, considerably more nationalist than Tudeh), and the Mujahedin-e Khalq (an Islamic socialist group), while differing in their goals for the country, were in agreement on this point. Each group, along with others in and out of the country, issued a stream of demands for a complete restructuring of the armed forces.[22] Obviously aware that dismantling the military would have given disproportionate influence to the groups in Iran that had refused to disarm, Khomeini and other leaders spoke out very early on the need for retaining a strong national military. "The army, police and gendarmerie are now in the service of Islam and the nation. The nation should support them, and do nothing that might discourage them or hurt their feelings. . . . I emphatically warn the Iranian nation that the government must have a strong national army with a mighty morale, so that the government will have the power to safeguard the country."[23]

Despite the best efforts of the new military leaders to exert control in this chaotic period, Western correspondents reported that the military was paralyzed by dissent and a breakdown in discipline, with soldiers vetoing the appointment of commanders and demanding the removal of senior officers.[24] To reduce the control of the officer corps over the organization, grassroots revolutionary councils composed of junior personnel sprang up at military installations throughout the country. Supported by diverse elements of the population that had an interest in reducing or eliminating the military, these councils severely crippled the concept of command authority. Officers who remained in the services were effectively intimidated by

21. Figures and percentages were obtained from analysis of reports of executions in FBIS, *Daily Report: MEA*, February–September 1979; and analysis of an American scholar on Iran, in correspondence with author, May 24, 1982.

22. See Shahram Chubin, "Leftist Forces in Iran," *Problems of Communism*, vol. 29 (July–August 1980), p. 19.

23. Speech by Ayatollah Khomeini on February 28, 1979, reported in FBIS, *Daily Report: MEA*, March 1, 1979, p. R2. For other strong statements in support of a national military, see statements by Khomeini in ibid., April 17, 1979, pp. R2–R3; October 9, 1979, p. R10; and December 31, 1979, p. 6. Other revolutionary leaders who supported Khomeini's call were Prime Minister Mehdi Bazargan (ibid., March 2, 1979, p. R4) and Ayatollah Kazem Shariatmadari (ibid., July 24, 1979, p. R7).

24. *New York Times*, February 20, 1979.

the councils and acquiesced to the weakening of their role.[25] It was, however, an untenable situation, one that Ayatollah Khomeini was forced to
address by April. "The army personnel are dutybound to observe army
discipline and the chain of command. . . . Disregarding these regulations
will lead to the weakness of the Islamic Army and will cause the breakdown
of discipline. . . . Disregarding this command is contrary to the revolution
and will be subject to reprimand."[26]

Despite such strong statements, the impasse persisted. In July the situation came to a head with a series of strikes by military technicians and
warrant officers at a number of air and ground force bases over the role of
the councils and the claim that both members of the former regime and
Americans were still in the military command structure. The confrontation
was successfully defused by Khomeini representatives, who called for Islamic unity for the sake of the revolution, but the discontent was not allevi-
ated.[27]

This strong support by Khomeini and others was influential in limiting
the effects of the purge in the early months of the Islamic republic. The
most important restraint, however, was the continuing political instability
in the country. As early as April 1 the provisional government was forced to
dispatch army troops to quell unrest in the northern province of Ma-
zandaran, a clear signal of its intention to use the regular armed forces to
maintain order.[28] By July demands for regional and tribal autonomy had
erupted in several areas, necessitating more troop deployments to Azerbaijan and Kurdistan in July and August and to Khuzestan in September.[29]
Although the military was not allowed to operate independently—that is,
without accompanying Revolutionary Guards—these deployments did give
it an opportunity to maintain its military skills and to regain some public
support.

As if to emphasize the controlled nature of the purge during this period,
as well as to rebuild public support for the military, Ayatollah Khomeini
declared an early amnesty for the army, police, and national police. The
Revolutionary Council followed this up much later by issuing its own wide-
ranging amnesty for members of the shah's armed and security services and

25. Edgar O'Ballance, "The Iranian Armed Forces," *Marine Corps Gazette*, August
1980, p. 48.
26. FBIS, *Daily Report: MEA*, April 17, 1979, p. R2.
27. Ibid., July 17, 1979, pp. R19–R21; July 24, 1979, pp. R6–R7; July 26, 1979, pp.
R6–R8.
28. Ibid., April 1, 1979, pp. R15–R16; and May 11, 1979, p. R3.
29. Ibid., July 26, 1979, p. R5; August 20, 1979, p. R2; and September 7, 1979, p. R1.

ordering an end to the accusations of antirevolutionary activity being lodged against individual servicemen. Ayatollah Khomeini endorsed this action: "The three branches of the armed forces are thus being pardoned, and I and the noble people forgive them."[30]

The second purge, which began in late September 1979, was of a very different kind, reflecting not only the popular demand for fundamental change within the military, but also the increased control exercised by Khomeini, which reduced the government's dependence on the military officers it had installed in command positions. Mostafa Chamran, the former deputy prime minister for revolutionary affairs in the provisional government, was appointed the first civilian minister of defense in late September. His primary qualification appears to have been his revolutionary zeal, which he displayed in early interviews with the Iranian press. "As far as I am concerned, the most important issue which must be addressed in the Defense Ministry . . . is the question of a purge in the army. Another important issue related to this purge . . . is the need to change the existing system in the army. . . . As far as we are concerned, the existing order is an order created and tailored by the satanic regime."[31]

In subsequent public statements Chamran outlined the thrust of his program for the military by identifying a series of problems and explaining how they would be corrected by his intended reorganization. The first of these was the need to alter the philosophical outlook of the organization. Expressing the view that the military had been created by Satan (the shah) to defend the interests of Zionism and imperialism, he said the true aim of the military was to safeguard the revolution and to guard Iran's independence. In order to achieve this redirection of effort, he indicated that a good deal of purging had to take place, based on revolutionary and Islamic criteria. The most important of these criteria were belief in Iran's independence and territorial integrity, belief in the Islamic revolution and in its leader, Ayatollah Khomeini, and obedience to and acceptance of the sovereignty of the government.[32]

Explicitly endorsing the concept of a strong national military establishment, Chamran then addressed the thorny issue of control within the armed forces: "By accepting the government's sovereignty, obedience to-

30. Ibid., July 10, 1979, p. R2. For the Revolutionary Council announcements, see *New York Times*, July 4, 1979; and FBIS, *Daily Report: MEA*, July 5, 1979, pp. R1–R3. Khomeini's earlier declaration is noted in FBIS, *Daily Report: MEA*, April 26, 1979, p. R9.

31. FBIS, *Daily Report: MEA*, October 1, 1979, p. R14.

32. Ibid., October 5, 1979, pp. R2–R3.

ward higher ranks becomes essential."[33] Ayatollah Khomeini reinforced the point shortly after Chamran took over: "It is essential, first, that the officers treat other sections in the armed forces with the utmost kindness and friendship, that the non-commissioned officers and soldiers obey their superiors, that they maintain the chain of command so as to make it possible for their job to be conducted successfully by maintaining order and discipline."[34]

Chamran approached the matter on Islamic grounds. Basing his philosophy on the Koranic dictum "and consult them about the issue in hand," he maintained that the councils existed merely to advise the commanders. The councils were free to express their views and give advice secure in the knowledge that the commanders would be duty-bound to pay attention to the proposals. "But the business of the command belongs to the commander and the councils will not have the right to interfere in the affairs of the command."[35] Over the next several months there were additional statements and pronouncements by various officials, enjoining military personnel to adhere to the chain of command and to reinstill discipline. By March the government even resorted to arresting the leaders of demonstrations. Despite this continuing effort, the councils and the more revolutionary members of the services persisted in their campaign, staging protest marches, demonstrations, and sit-ins.[36] The issue remained unresolved until the military invasion by Iraq kindled a sense of nationalism, which swept it aside.

Finally, Chamran took up the proper organization of the Islamic military. "We believe that the entire Iranian nation should become the soldiers of the revolution. . . . The army should also be turned into a specialized and modern technical cadre."[37] A few weeks later, when the hostage crisis erupted and military retaliation by the United States seemed probable, Ayatollah Khomeini incorporated this theme and called for the creation of an "Army of Twenty Million" to combat imperialism. This call to arms of virtually anyone willing and able to carry a gun resulted in the establish-

33. Ibid.
34. FBIS, *Daily Report: MEA*, October 9, 1979, p. R10.
35. Ibid., October 5, 1979, p. R3.
36. Ibid., supplement 062, March 12, 1980, p. 19. For statements of Islamic officials regarding chain of command, see FBIS, *Daily Report: MEA*, December 5, 1979, pp. R11–R12 (Bazargan); ibid., supplement 050, December 31, 1979, p. 6 (Khomeini); supplement 016, January 16, 1980, p. 12 (Deputy Defense Minister Khamene'i); and supplement 046, February 20, 1980, pp. 4–5 (Bani-Sadr).
37. FBIS, *Daily Report: MEA*, October 9, 1979, p. R13.

ment of a staff for mobilization of the people and widespread weapons training courses in schools, factories, and on television.[38] Although there was a tendency in the West to regard this effort merely as part of the anti-U.S. campaign being waged by the Iranian government, it really represented a significant organizational step for the armed forces of Iran. Providing a large pool of semitrained personnel on which to draw during military contingencies eliminated the need to maintain the army at the prerevolutionary size. As early as May 1979 the government had indicated its desire to cut the army in half,[39] but not until the creation of the Army of Twenty Million did it have the necessary manpower for defense that would safely allow keeping the army at the lower level.

Having established his goals for the military, Chamran quickly implemented his promised purge. Under the guidelines of a bill passed by the Revolutionary Council covering the purging of the entire government, Chamran established a series of committees in the Ministry of Defense and the armed services to review the records of military and civilian personnel associated with the ministry. Those who fitted the criteria for purging were dismissed from the services, but were "free and entitled to enjoy human dignity."[40] By February 1980 the deputy defense minister, Hojjat ol-Eslam Seyyid' Ali Khamene'i, claimed that some 6,000 people had been purged and promised further dismissals.[41] As President Abol Hassan Bani-Sadr ruefully acknowledged after the Iraqi invasion, that promise was fulfilled. By that time 12,000 people had been purged, 10,000 of them from the army.[42]

The Islamic government's concern about counterrevolutionary activity was heightened as a result of the U.S. attempt to rescue the hostages in April 1980. Because the raid was strongly suspected of being a cover for an attempted coup by the Iranian military, a commission was formed to look

38. Unlike the Revolutionary Guards, who are committed revolutionaries, the Army of Twenty Million is a militia organized to fight invaders, not internal enemies of the revolution, which is the province of the Guards.

For Khomeini's call to arms, see FBIS, *Daily Report: MEA*, November 27, 1979, p. R8. For statements on the Army of Twenty Million, see ibid., December 3, 1979, pp. R23–R24; and December 5, 1979, p. R11; ibid., supplement 043, December 19, 1979, p. 31; and supplement 037, December 21, 1979, pp. R24–R25.

39. FBIS, *Daily Report: MEA*, May 4, 1979, p. R1.

40. Interview with the chief of staff of the Iranian army reported in ibid., supplement 042, February 14, 1980, pp. 22–24.

41. Ibid., supplement 048, February 22, 1980, p. 9.

42. FBIS, *Daily Report: South Asia*, October 15, 1980, p. 112. (Hereafter FBIS, *Daily Report: SAS*.)

into the raid and the actions of all Iranian military personnel at the time. After the air force bombed the abandoned helicopters in the desert, effectively destroying some physical evidence of the raid, the air force chief of staff, General Bahman Bagheri, was especially suspect, but without direct evidence, the commission could do nothing.[43]

After an attempted coup was thwarted at the army garrison in Piranshahr along the Iraqi-Azerbaijani border in June, the government felt secure enough to take action against some of the senior officers suspected of complicity in the U.S. raid. This relatively small group had remained loyal to the shah throughout the revolution and had rallied to Khomeini only after the first purge began, when they had professed loyalty to Khomeini and the revolution and been given command positions. In the atmosphere of the second purge, however, especially after the U.S. raid, these officers were considered dangerous. When a more extensive plot was uncovered in July, the government used it as justification for a wholesale move against the remaining officers in this group, the most notable being General Bagheri.[44] Although the July coup attempt indicated widespread coordination among persons in the services, there is little evidence that all of those dismissed were directly involved. The significance of the coup attempts was not that they occurred, but the way the government used them as excuses to weed out potentially serious opposition in the military.

The Effects of the Purge

The first purge had eliminated only the highest level of the military leadership, those considered most loyal to the shah, and those guilty of specific counterrevolutionary crimes. The second purge concentrated on lower echelons, those whose loyalty was suspect though they were not guilty of serious crimes against the revolution.[45] Suspicion was aroused by previous association with Americans, training in the United States, relationships with those already purged, or other such factors. Since the warrant officers and military technicians were considered to have been a major

43. Interview with Revolutionary Council member Hashemi Rafsanjani, reported in FBIS, *Daily Report: SAS*, July 14, 1980, pp. I10–I22, especially pp. I10, I13, and I18. See also Bani-Sadr interview in ibid., July 3, 1980, pp. I7–I9.

44. For information on the June plot, see FBIS, *Daily Report: SAS*, June 24, 1980, pp. I15–I17; and June 25, 1980, pp. I15–I17. For the July plot, see ibid., July 11, 1980, pp. I5–I8; July 14, 1980, pp. I1–I22; July 17, 1980, pp. I1–I4; and July 18, 1980, pp. I4–I8.

45. FBIS, *Daily Report: MEA*, October 5, 1979, p. R2.

revolutionary force in the final days of the revolution and the conscripts in general to have been victims of the shah's military policies, it can be surmised that the purge fell most heavily on the officer corps and, to a lesser extent, the cadre of noncommissioned officers. To obtain some sense of how the purge affected the officer corps, it is first necessary to describe the distribution of officers within it.

Since precise data are not available, an initial estimate of the size and distribution of the Imperial Iranian officer corps was made using U.S. figures, on the grounds that the Iranian military was modeled closely after the American military. In 1979 the percentage of officers in the U.S. armed forces was as follows: Army, 12.8; Navy, 11.9; and Air Force, 17.2.[46] If the American percentages are applied to a 1979 estimate of 415,000 men in the Iranian military (285,000 army, 30,000 navy, and 100,000 air force),[47] the following officer strengths would result: army, 36,500; navy, 3,600; and air force, 17,300 (see table 1).

The purge affected all the services, but its most serious effect was on the army. As Bani-Sadr pointed out, 10,000 of those purged were from the army, meaning that only 2,000 were eliminated from the navy, air force, and civilian agencies combined. This imbalance indicates the general attitude toward the individual services. The navy had not been an active participant in the military government instituted by the shah in the closing days of the revolution, nor had it been involved in the government's response to the riots and street demonstrations. It therefore emerged from the revolution relatively unscathed. Rear Admiral Madani, the first commander of the navy after the revolution, had been able to maintain and improve the public image of his service by using navy men to enforce Islamic rule in Khuzestan, where he was governor. The air force too had a good revolutionary reputation based on the actions of its members in opposing the military authorities in the closing days of the revolution.

The group in the army most affected by the purge was the officer corps. Although a number of noncommissioned officers from the Imperial Guard and other cadre units were eliminated, the officer corps' association with the shah and with the American military undoubtedly made it the primary target. The officer corps was also held responsible for the deaths of many revolutionaries. It is therefore reasonable to assume that the vast majority of those eliminated were officers, and for the purposes of analysis, a figure

46. U.S. Department of Defense, *Selected Manpower Statistics, FY 1979*, pp. 73, 75.
47. International Institute of Strategic Studies, *The Military Balance, 1979–1980*, p. 39.

Table 1. *Estimated Distribution of Officers in the Iranian Armed Services*

Service and rank	Percentage, U.S. forces	Numerical strength, Iranian forces[a]
Army		
General (all)	0.5	180[b]
Colonel	5.3	1,900
Lieutenant colonel	13.1	4,800
Major	19.0	6,900
Captain	31.2	11,400
1st lieutenant	15.5	5,700
2nd lieutenant	15.4	5,600
Total	100.0	36,500
Navy		
Admiral (all)	0.4	140[b]
Captain	6.2	200
Commander	12.7	500
Lieutenant commander	20.1	700
Lieutenant	29.5	1,100
Lieutenant junior grade	16.1	600
Ensign	15.0	500
Total	100.0	3,600
Air Force		
General (all)	0.4	70[b]
Colonel	5.4	900
Lieutenant colonel	13.1	2,300
Major	18.8	3,200
Captain	38.7	6,700
1st lieutenant	9.8	1,700
2nd lieutenant	13.8	2,400
Total	100.0	17,300

Source: U.S. Department of Defense, *Selected Manpower Statistics, FY 1979*, p. 82. Percentages extrapolated; numerical strengths verified by expatriate senior officers of the Imperial Iranian Military now living in the United States.
a. Figures are rounded.
b. Some sources indicate significantly more general officers.

of 10 percent of those purged is allowed for the noncommissioned officers and other cadre.

The remaining 9,000 men removed represent some 23 percent of the army officer corps, but the officers most likely to have been targets were concentrated in the field grades of major through colonel, of whom there were almost 14,000 (table 1). If only 50 percent of these officers were from this group, this would represent a purge of about one-third of the field grade officers. Applying the more likely figure of 80 percent would mean the removal of over half such officers, with a devastating effect on the army's ability to conduct combat operations.

The Islamic Military

By the end of the summer of 1980 the purges had been very successful in the army. As late as the first week of September, Bani-Sadr spoke of the need for continued change in the military to bring it into line with the goals of the Islamic republic, indicating that purges were to continue.[48] However, he claims that, at about the same time, intermediaries in Paris passed him a copy of a purported Iraqi plan to invade southwest Iran. Initially skeptical of its authenticity, he became convinced only after he verified some of the information it contained, such as the massive military buildup along the Iranian border. Recognizing that the army was in no shape to meet such a threat, he says that he warned Prime Minister Rajai and others of it. Because he was engaged in a major struggle for domestic political power with Rajai and the other radicals of the dominant Islamic Republican party (IRP), he was unable to make the other Iranian leaders believe in the impending invasion. As a result, nothing was done to prepare for it.[49]

All of the Iranian armed forces were unprepared for war, both organizationally and because their equipment had been allowed to deteriorate. Because its leadership had been ravaged by a combination of revolutionary zeal and suspicion, the army was clearly in the worst shape; the air force and the navy had been able to retain some operational effectiveness. Although their leaders had been replaced during the purge, their basic command structures remained intact, a factor that would prove significant in the early weeks of the war. Perhaps more important, however, was the relationship each had developed with the clerical regime and its paramilitary arm, the Revolutionary Guards. Aside from the revolutionary reputation each service had maintained, which tended to moderate some of the antimilitary bias of the regime, the air force and the navy possessed military skills that the Guards could not hope to master. Weapons training and combat experience against the Kurds and other dissident groups may have given them some competence in ground operations but hardly qualified them for air or naval warfare. For this reason, as long as the commanders of

48. FBIS, *Daily Report: SAS*, September 8, 1980, p. 110.
49. Eric Roleau, *Le Monde*, January 6, 1981, translated in FBIS, *Daily Report: SAS*, January 7, 1981, p. 120.

the air force and the navy were sufficiently revolutionary and Islamic in orientation, the regime was inclined to allow them a degree of latitude in their operations that it would not afford the army.

The evolution of the military into an effective fighting force and its final emergence as an Islamic institution can be traced through three distinct phases of the war. The first, in which the Iraqi forces were on the offensive, lasted some seven weeks. The second, from the beginning of November until the summer of 1981, was a period of stalemate on the battlefield—the Iraqis were dug into defensive positions and the Iranian effort was hampered by the power struggle in Tehran. In the third period, from September 1981 through the spring of 1982, Iranian forces seized the initiative and scored a series of victories that drove the Iraqis out of Iran.

The first phase was a period of mobilization and deployment marked by ad hoc tactics and a total lack of coordination. Each of the services planned and conducted its own actions against the enemy, which resulted in a predictable lack of strategic success. Throughout this period, the Iranian army did not play a major role in the fighting. Despite Bani-Sadr's foreknowledge of the Iraqi attack, at the outbreak of the war the army was not positioned in strength along the Iraqi border: at the direction of Chamran, most of it was engaged in operations against Kurdish dissidents and deployed along the northern border to guard against an "imminent" invasion from the Soviet Union.[50] Small units of regular troops were stationed throughout Khuzestan, but for the most part the initial defense of the region was to be the responsibility of the Revolutionary Guards and the local militias. Shortly after the war began, Western reporters questioned Bani-Sadr about the absence of the army from the battle front in Khuzestan. He acknowledged that the Revolutionary Guards and the local population were doing most of the fighting against the Iraqis on the ground and said, "Our ground forces have encountered much more serious problems than the other sections of the armed forces . . . we decided to send only one division to the south in order not to further expose our forces to fire from Iraqi heavy artillery which is close by."[51]

Despite the strategic decision not to deploy the army in force to support the civilian defenders of the major population centers of the south, individual regular units scattered throughout the region played an important tactical role. Because of a lack of command coordination, however, these units

50. Ibid.
51. Eric Roleau, *Le Monde*, October 11, 1980, translated in FBIS, *Daily Report: SAS*, October 15, 1980, p. 112.

did not mesh well with the Revolutionary Guards, and reports reached the West of bitter rivalries between units of regular troops and Guards in Khuzestan. Without explicit directions from Tehran on command arrangements, chaos prevailed. When either a regular soldier or a Guard assumed command of a mixed unit, the men of the other organization refused to follow his orders.[52] This unsatisfactory situation persisted throughout the initial phase of the war, resulting in indecisive strategy and inconclusive actions. That the Iranians were able to put up as effective a defense on the ground as they did despite the lack of coordination was due to the intangible components of Islamic fervor and Iranian nationalism.

For devout Muslims, to die while doing battle in the cause of Islam is martyrdom, which assures immediate entry into heaven. This belief sustained the Revolutionary Guards and other equally devout fighters on the front with Iraq and gave them the courage necessary to withstand repeated assaults and nearly incessant shelling. Although Islamic fervor could not provide the less devout with the same spiritual sustenance, the desire to defend the Iranian homeland (nationalism) enabled them to put up a tenacious defense against the Iraqi invaders. These two factors, which generally had not been recognized in Western analyses of Iran's military capabilities against Iraq,[53] proved decisive in the first phase of the evolution of the Iranian military during the war. Whether one believes that the Iraqi drive was halted because of Iraqi ineptness or because Saddam Hussein was unwilling to accept the high casualty rates that would have been necessary to clear the major population centers of Abadan, Ahwaz, and Dezful, it is generally conceded that the fierce Iranian ground defense was a major factor in the Iraqis' decision to go on the defensive and fortify their positions.[54]

In contrast to the restrained employment of the army in the first phase, the air force began intensive operations against Iraqi targets almost immediately, rapidly expanding to a sortie rate that astonished most observers. Flying planes that in other air forces would have been grounded for inadequate maintenance, Iranian pilots staged a number of spectacular raids against a variety of targets throughout Iraq.[55] While acknowledging that achieving the high sortie rate was remarkable, U.S. analysts criticized the

52. *New York Times*, October 24, 1980.
53. See, for example, *New York Times*, April 13, September 23, and September 25, 1980.
54. See, for example, Edgar O'Ballance, "The Iraqi-Iranian War: The First Round," *Parameters: Journal of the US Army War College*, vol. 11 (March 1981), p. 56; and *The Economist*, May 9, 1981, p. 32.
55. *New York Times*, September 24, September 25, and October 15, 1980.

choice of targets on the grounds that they were chosen for political or psychological value rather than military utility. This, they maintained, reflected the initiative of individual pilots, all of whom had been trained in the United States, and indicated the lack of a command structure, intelligence, and communications.[56]

The unstated assumption was that if the air force had had a command structure it would have chosen to conduct operations of more direct military value, such as flying close air support for the Iranian ground troops or conducting combat air patrols over the battle front to prevent the incursion of Iraqi aircraft into Iranian air space. The assumption, however, was invalid, since the air force emerged from the purges with a command structure in place, although it was decidedly Islamic in orientation. The decision to strike lightly defended targets away from the battlefield of maximum political and psychological value was undoubtedly a command decision based on a realistic assessment of the training of the pilots involved as well as a desire to extract the maximum value from limited assets. Operations such as close air support and combat air patrol require a high degree of training and coordination, both of which were lacking during the initial phase of the war. Furthermore, when the Iraqis invaded, their forward elements were protected by an array of antiaircraft missiles and guns. Striking psychologically vulnerable targets within Iraq well away from the front forced the Iraqis to pull some of that air defense equipment back to defend vulnerable areas in the rear.[57]

Like the air force, the navy went on the offensive very quickly, engaging the Iraqis three times in the first ten days of the war, at Basra, Fao, and Mina al-Bakr, Iraq's offshore oil terminal.[58] After these engagements, there was speculation in the West that the navy might become a critical component in the war, but it retired from direct combat to undertake a limited mission of interrupting Iraqi commerce. It accomplished this by maintaining patrols in the Strait of Hormuz and the Persian Gulf areas designated as war zones by the Islamic government.

During the initial phase, two major weaknesses of the Iranian military become clear: operational limitations resulting from the shortage of repair parts and military supplies and ineffectiveness resulting from the lack of command coordination. Although Iranian technicians became adept at cannibalizing damaged or inoperative equipment to keep at least some

56. Ibid., October 3, 1980.
57. Ibid., October 19, 1980.
58. Ibid., September 25 and September 30, 1980.

equipment operational, by the end of October operations had been reduced significantly for the sections of the military that were dependent on periodic maintenance. All the armed forces were affected to some degree, but the service most affected was the air force, which was forced to scale back drastically the number of daily sorties as a direct result of the repair parts problem.[59] The problem was to plague the Iranians throughout the war since few nations were willing to sell them military equipment, even after the release of the American hostages in January 1981.

A much more serious problem was the ineffectiveness on the battlefield caused by the lack of command coordination. Aside from the rivalries that had developed between the army and the Revolutionary Guards during the purges, the rancor and disharmony on the battlefield were a reflection of the political quarrels taking place in Tehran, where President Bani-Sadr, the leader of the minority secular forces of the government, was locked in a bitter struggle for power with Prime Minister Muhammad Ali Rajai and the cleric-dominated IRP. At the beginning of the war, Bani-Sadr attempted to monopolize the planning by holding meetings, as commander-in-chief, with his military commanders in an American-style national security council.[60] By the second week of the war, however, the power struggle with Rajai prevented this group from functioning effectively. It was not until Ayatollah Khomeini intervened that the Supreme Defense Council (SDC) began to function. The final composition of the panel was a setback for Bani-Sadr since a number of hardliners from the IRP were included, but for the military the first meeting of the expanded group was the initial step toward command coordination.[61] Because of the ideological split, the SDC was unable to reach agreement on many issues, but they at least named a single commander to control operations in Khuzestan.[62] The mistrust and animosity between the defending forces on the front, however, continued unabated.

The ideological struggle in Tehran dominated the second phase of the war. Although the struggle was manifested in a seven-month stalemate on the battle front, significant changes took place during this period that improved the effectiveness of the military and moved it closer to the status of an Islamic institution. The army had been redeployed to the Khuzestan region to assume responsibility for the fighting there, but little effort was

59. Ibid., November 1, 1980.
60. FBIS, *Daily Report: SAS*, September 22, 1980, p. 13; and September 29, 1980, p. 110.
61. Ibid., October 15, 1980, p. 11.
62. Ibid., October 31, 1980, p. 12.

made to conduct coordinated operations with the Revolutionary Guards and local militia. Although they were colocated, the army and the Guards conducted virtually separate wars. Each had its own general staff, intelligence service, and public relations office. Both General Valiollah Fallahi, the acting chief of the joint staff, and Morteza Rezaiyeh, the leader of the Revolutionary Guards, were members of the SDC, but the political battle precluded effective cooperation between them and between their subordinates. The mistrust was reinforced by the way the Guards were used: they were positioned behind the regular troops, ostensibly to prevent the troops from withdrawing or deserting.[63]

Once the war settled into stalemate, President Bani-Sadr and his domestic antagonists used it as a tool in their power struggle. As commander-in-chief, Bani-Sadr attempted to preempt his critics by moving to Dezful where he could direct the war without interference. While at the front, he spent much of his time visiting army units and issuing public statements that constantly emphasized the strengths and accomplishments of the army and ignored the disputes in Tehran.[64] By aligning himself with the newly popular military, Bani-Sadr could hope to strengthen his position in the power struggle by drawing on the pro-military mood of the public. High-ranking clerics and other members of the IRP, in contrast, lauded the efforts of the Revolutionary Guards and denigrated the military.[65] When asked whether he was forcing the army into the background for tactical reasons or as a matter of religious ideology, Ayatollah Montazeri, the designated successor to Ayatollah Khomeini, responded, "We can only defend the country with a force we trust."[66]

Even though Bani-Sadr was initially successful in building support for his position by casting himself in the role of commander-in-chief, he was soon outflanked by his rivals as they began to call for the unity of all of the forces on the battlefield, presumably under the leadership of the Revolutionary Guards and their clerical supporters.[67] Senior military officers maintained that such unity had already been achieved, but a series of

63. Edgar O'Ballance, "The Iran-Iraq War," *Islamic World Defence*, vol. 1 (Autumn 1981), p. 16.

64. See, for example, FBIS, *Daily Report: SAS*, November 4, 1980, p. 112; and November 20, 1980, pp. I1–I4; and Eric Roleau, *Le Monde*, January 7, 1981, translated in FBIS, *Daily Report: SAS*, January 9, 1981, p. I5.

65. Roleau, in FBIS, *Daily Report: SAS*, January 9, 1981, p. I5.

66. FBIS, *Daily Report: SAS*, November 18, 1980, p. I5.

67. See statement by Rajai in ibid., December 12, 1980, p. I2.

statements and appeals from Ayatollah Khomeini indicated that it was illusory.[68]

A major concern of the hardliners and a basic consideration in the unity theme was the close relationship developing between the president and the military. The clerical establishment feared that Bani-Sadr, by spending so much of his time on the front lines with the troops, was isolating the army from the influence of the Islamic revolution. Underlying this was the fear that allowing this isolation to develop increased the possibility of a coup by disaffected officers. Ayatollah Montazeri warned of "the dangers of a separation arising between the army and the Moslem Iranian nation, the revolutionary institutions and the militant clergy," and called on the authorities to prevent the "infiltration of elements that do not believe in the Islamic revolution into sensitive positions within the armed forces."[69] In an interview with a West German reporter, Rajai defined this group as only "a small segment of the military and an infinitesimal group of so-called intellectuals oriented toward the West, headed by Bani-Sadr."[70] Fear of a military coup was not confined to the clerical regime. Bani-Sadr received a warning from the Mujahedin-e Khalq in the form of an open letter condemning the commanders of the army and warning that hatred was building against the regime in the armed forces and that even clerical dress was despised by the military.[71]

To counteract this concern, the Supreme Defense Council appointed permanent representatives to supervise the various fronts. Bani-Sadr objected to their appointment, but the SDC, which had recently been expanded to include more hardliners, ignored his protests. The effect of this was to lessen the singular influence Bani-Sadr had over the military as commander-in-chief.[72] The regime also issued a series of statements supporting the military and emphasizing the ties between it and the clerics. The most comprehensive of these was an unattributed commentary on Radio Tehran that recalled the weakness and disorganization of the military after the fall of the shah and stated, "The imam of the nation and the aware clergy resuscitated the moribund army and with the cooperation of the

68. Khomeini's statements in ibid., December 8, 1980, p. 16; December 15, 1980, p. 115; January 2, 1981, p. 18; and January 21, 1981, p. 138. For a senior officer's view, see statement by General Fallahi in ibid., December 8, 1980, p. 15.

69. *Financial Times*, January 10, 1981.

70. FBIS, *Daily Report: SAS*, January 5, 1981, p. 116.

71. *Financial Times*, January 10, 1981.

72. Roleau, *Le Monde*, January 7, 1981, translated in FBIS, *Daily Report: SAS*, January 9, 1981, p. 16.

committed commanders reorganized it." Claiming that the imam and the aware clergy had "always supported" the armed forces and thus had won the support of the "Muslim masses" for them, the commentary declared that the military should realize that the "imam and the forces following the line of the imam" were "the true supporters and sincere friends of the armed forces."[73] Even Ayatollah Khomeini registered his concern about the possibility of isolating the military with a series of strong statements about the clerical ties to the armed forces.[74]

The result of this ideological tug of war was a stalemate on the battle-field. Although the army did not have the strength to repel the invaders by itself, the radical elements of the government increased the pressure on Bani-Sadr to begin his long-promised counteroffensive.[75] In early January he ordered the army and air force to conduct a coordinated operation to relieve Iraqi pressure on the vital transportation center of Dezful. Buoyed up by the initial success of the attack, he sent a letter to Ayatollah Khomeini claiming great victories,[76] but when the Iraqis outflanked and defeated the Iranian forces several days later, he was forced to back off, vowing to fight on despite the high cost of holding out.[77] As time passed with no further significant military action, however, his opponents increased the intensity and frequency of their political attacks on him. A highly publicized air raid on an air base deep inside Iraq in early April may have been another attempt by Bani-Sadr to use the military to silence his domestic critics, but if so, it did not succeed.[78] Even though the raid was a significant achievement, Bani-Sadr was unable to capitalize on it as he had on the January offensive. In the earlier instance Bani-Sadr had been widely viewed as the politician with the most influence over the military, and he was thus able to derive some direct political benefit from the military success. By April, however, his influence had been undermined by the presence of the clerical representatives on the SDC. Therefore, when the military

73. FBIS, *Daily Report: SAS*, January 16, 1981, p. 110. See also ibid., January 19, 1981, pp. 132–133.

74. See Khomeini statements in ibid., December 8, 1980, p. 16; January 13, 1981, p. 14; and January 30, 1981, p. 13.

75. See, for example, statement by Ayatollah Beheshti in ibid., January 7, 1981, pp. 116–117.

76. *New York Times*, January 6, 1981.

77. Ibid., January 10, 1981. For analysis of the offensive, see ibid., January 8, 1981; *The Economist*, May 9, 1981, p. 32; and O'Ballance, "The Iran-Iraq War," p. 18.

78. *Middle East Intelligence Survey*, vol. 8 (January 1–15, 1981), pp. 147–48.

executed an extremely successful raid, he gained little personal political benefit from it.

As the political attacks on him escalated, Bani-Sadr's influence over the military waned still further. Although he had been the most prominent secular proponent of the military during the war, when Ayatollah Khomeini dismissed him, the military did not come to his defense, which clearly indicated the influence the clerical regime had gained over the armed forces and laid the groundwork for the emergence of the military as an Islamic institution. The regime, however, was not sufficiently confident of its control to use the military against the Mujahedin-e Kalq during the civil disturbances that raged in the months following Bani-Sadr's dismissal.

In addition to the shift in control of the military from secular to Islamic influence, a more subtle though equally important change occurred on the battlefield during this period. As the January offensive had made clear, coordinated action by the military forces alone was not enough to defeat the Iraqis; cooperation with the popular forces was a necessity. In the months following the offensive, the army and the Guards began to reach an uneasy accommodation. Although their individual public statements continued to stress the actions of their own organizations, references to joint operations began to appear. By April it was clear that some success had been achieved in such operations, though on a small scale.[79] There was no love lost between the Guards and the army, but at least a grudging respect was established. The first significant test of this new working relationship was a successful effort in late May to dislodge the Iraqi forces from the Allaho Akbar heights to the west of Susangerd. This action established a pattern of cooperation on which future operations were based.

Once the ideological struggle in Tehran was concluded and the street battles resulting from its conclusion were nearly finished, the stalemate on the battlefield was resolved. During the third phase of the war, the military seized the operational initiative and emerged as an effective fighting force. The major factors that allowed this final transformation were (1) elimination of the conflicting guidance given the military as a result of the power struggle; (2) resolution, however tenuous, of the bitter disputes between the army and the Revolutionary Guards, which resulted in increased cooperation and joint operations; and (3) improved tactics, intelligence, and planning on the part of the military.

The lifting of the siege of Abadan in late September demonstrated the

79. FBIS, *Daily Report: SAS*, April 6, 1981, pp. 11–13; and April 8, 1981, pp. 11–12.

working relationship that had been established between the army and the Guards. On September 27 the Iranians capitalized on intelligence that pinpointed weaknesses in the Iraqi defenses around Abadan and, in a surprise night attack, sent commando teams through the Iraqi lines to hit specific targets. They followed up with a direct attack, using both army and Revolutionary Guard units augmented by popular forces of the Army of Twenty Million, which forced the Iraqis to retreat across the Karun River, effectively lifting the siege of Abadan.[80] Three days before the attack, the commanders of the Guards corps invited the senior commanders of the armed forces to a meeting in Tehran to "deal with certain problems, including the acceleration of the pace of the war, ending the war, more practical coordination between the corps and the army and long term plans."[81] The clear implication of the September 24 meeting is that the Guards were sharing intelligence with their military counterparts and putting the finishing touches on their plans.

Although the Iranian forces won a significant victory, they were unable to follow it with a quick second strike, which indicates both that they had still not overcome the weakness noted at the outset of the war, inadequate logistical support, and that they did not have an exploitable reserve force. The battle did show, however, that the capabilities of the Iranian planners had greatly improved. The tactics used were not complicated, but they were substantially better than had been previously noted. It is significant that even the Guards, after first giving credit for the victory to the power of God, listed adherence to a well-conceived plan as a reason for the victory.[82] But the lack of a reserve force meant a lost opportunity to wreak havoc on the temporarily disorganized Iraqi forces, although without the logistical support necessary to sustain such an operation, any Iranian force north of the Karun River would have been seriously imperiled.

The magnitude of the improvements in military planning was shown shortly after the battle when General Fallahi, the architect of Iran's resistance to the Iraqi invasion, was killed in the September 29 crash of a C-130 returning to Tehran from Ahvaz. Killed with him were the acting commander of the Revolutionary Guards, the defense minister, and a former

80. Ibid., September 28, 1981, pp. I1–I2.
81. Ibid., September 25, 1981, p. I7.
82. For Iranian reports of the battle, see ibid., September 28, 1981, pp. I1–I3; and September 29, 1981, pp. I1–I6. For representative Western reporting and commentary, see *Washington Post*, September 28, 1981; *New York Times*, September 28, 1981; *The Economist*, October 3, 1981, pp. 63–64; *Strategy Week*, October 5–11, 1981, p. 4; and *Newsweek*, March 8, 1982, p. 36.

defense minister, as well as a number of other military and paramilitary personnel.[83] Despite these serious losses, the planning and coordination that characterized the Abadan operation were not lost. They were, in fact, improved.

The military operation that proved this point took place in late November in the region surrounding Bostan, a small village northwest of Susangerd, near the Iraqi border. "Operation Jerusalem Way," as it was called by the Iranians, was a significant shift in tactics. Unable to obtain enough parts for their armored vehicles, they turned to an infantry strategy, one that relied on individual fervor to overcome staggering military odds.[84] Faced with well-entrenched Iraqi troops protected by minefields, the Iranians sent forerunners, who were ready to sacrifice themselves by blowing up mines with their bodies, through the minefields and followed them with waves of fighters. Though expensive in human terms, these tactics were very effective. They demoralized the defending Iraqis, who could not respond effectively to hosts of Iranians willing to die. The result was an Iranian victory that drove a wedge into the Iraqi lines and set up the succeeding battles the following spring.[85]

There are conflicting reports about the Bostan operation. The regime fostered the notion that the Revolutionary Guards and the popular forces were the primary forces in the battle. While not openly denigrating the efforts of the regular army, spokesmen for the regime glossed over its contribution in statements extolling the self-sacrifice and morale of the irregular forces. The Western media, lacking adequate access to corroborating information, are dependent on pronouncements of the regime for much of their information and have repeated this story.[86] Although precise data are unavailable, portions of the U.S. intelligence community believe that the Revolutionary Guards were assigned merely a sector of the operation, where they admittedly performed well.[87] The regime's public award of credit for the victory to the Guards, however, implicitly denies the army's

    83. FBIS, *Daily Report: SAS*, September 30, 1981, p. 11.
    84. Ibid., pp. 11–12; and *Strategy Week*, October 12–18, 1981, p. 4.
    85. *Washington Post*, January 16, 1982; and *Financial Times*, September 15, 1981.
    86. For the Iranian reports of the fighting, see FBIS, *Daily Report: SAS*, November 30, 1981, pp. 11–14; December 7, 1981, pp. 13–14; and December 9, 1981, pp. 18–19. For representative Western reporting, see *Washington Post*, November 30, 1981; *New York Times*, November 30, 1981; and *The Middle East Reporter*, December 5, 1981, p. 6.
    87. See, for example, statement by Prime Minister Mir-Hoseyn Musavi in FBIS, *Daily Report: SAS*, December 7, 1981, pp. 13–14. For representative Western reporting, see *Middle East Economic Digest*, December 18, 1981, p. 45; and *Newsweek*, March 8, 1982, p. 36.

role in the war. Although the army was able to establish a tenuous but effective working relationship with the Guards, there was little evidence to this point in the war that the professional soldiers had done more than temporarily suppress their animosity and disdain for the youthful Guards, whom they sometimes referred to as "SSlam," an obvious reference to Hitler's notorious *Schutzstaffel*, or elite guard.[88] A Swedish correspondent touring the front at about this time confirmed this, having discovered virtual contempt for the Guards among the professional ranks.[89]

Iranian forces maintained contact with the Iraqis over the winter in small skirmishes, but they did not launch another major offensive until early spring. In February, apparently aware that the Iranians were involved in a heavy buildup for that offensive, the Iraqis initiated a series of probing attacks. They had some limited tactical success but were unable to disrupt the Iranian plans.[90]

When it started in late March, the Iranian offensive, code named "Undeniable Victory," was the largest and most complex Iranian effort in the war until then. With more than 100,000 regular troops, at least 30,000 Guards, and the same number of popular forces from the Army of Twenty Million, the Iranians launched a three-phase operation that broke the back of the Iraqi resistance in Khuzestan. The attack began with a surprise nighttime infiltration of Iranian armored units well behind the Iraqi front lines, where they concentrated on isolating the front-line soldiers by attacking headquarters units and destroying communications centers. They followed this up with human-wave assaults on the isolated and confused Iraqis. In a combined arms operation that for the first time in the war made effective use of artillery, fighter-bomber aircraft, helicopters, and armor in support of massive infantry assaults, the Iranians decimated three full Iraqi armored and mechanized divisions, capturing between 15,000 and 20,000 men in a classic pincer movement.[91]

With this action, the Iranian military demonstrated that it had finally

88. Author's interview (unclassified) with a Department of State analyst, February 10, 1982.

89. *Svenska Dagbladet*, October 24, 1981, p. 5, translated in FBIS, *Daily Report: SAS*, October 29, 1981, pp. 15–17.

90. *New York Times*, February 11, 1982; and *Washington Post*, March 1, 1982.

91. For Iranian reporting of the offensive, see FBIS, *Daily Report: SAS*, March 22, 1982, pp. I17–I20; March 23, 1982, pp. I1–I6; March 25, 1982, pp. I1–I3; March 29, 1982, pp. I8–I11; March 30, 1982, pp. I1–I3; and March 31, 1982, pp. I3–I4. For representative Western reporting and commentary, see *Washington Post*, March 29, 30, and 31, and April 1, 1982. See also *New York Times*, April 7, 1982.

become a well-led, technically efficient fighting force. Maneuvering five divisions on the battlefield would not be a complicated operation for a modern army with a competent, well-trained leadership, but for Iran's army, which had been ravaged by the second purge, it was a major undertaking. That it performed as well as it did is indicative of the vast improvements that had been made in planning, coordination, and execution.

Another indication of its qualitative advances was the amount of time required for Iran to regroup its forces for the next assault. In the preceding operations, about two months had been necessary to reassemble and concentrate enough force to launch another major offensive. After the Dezful operation, however, only one month was needed. On April 30, in a replay of the previous battle, the Iranians initiated "Operation Holy City," designed as the final push to drive the Iraqis out of southern Khuzestan altogether. Using surprise attacks, infantry and armor infiltration, human waves, and coordinated arms in support of tenacious regular and irregular forces, the Iranian military forced the Iraqis back across the border, ending the occupation of southern Iran.[92]

Western correspondents readmitted to Iran after these battles noted a shift in the attitude of the military. Where formerly the professional soldiers had been openly contemptuous of the Revolutionary Guards and other popular forces, in the spring of 1982 the soldiers tended to describe their actions in Islamic rather than secular terms.[93] While it is clear that such statements could have reflected merely the desire of the speakers to appear sufficiently committed before foreigners, that they were uttered at all shows a significant change in the way the military perceives itself. Since the ouster of Bani-Sadr, the military has been subjected to the tight control and continual influence of the clergy in their roles as advisers and representatives of the regime, without a corresponding influence from a secular source. Also, the military officers chosen for command positions were young, ambitious, motivated, and dedicated to Islam.[94] Together, these two influences "Islamized" the war for the professional military, or at least convinced them that it was necessary to address it in Islamic terms. Add to this that a large portion of the military, including warrant officers, technicians, conscripts, and even some officers, is sincerely committed to the Islamic goals of the regime, and the statements given to Western correspondents reflect a realistic assessment of the current political climate, both

92. *Washington Post*, May 7, 9, and 26, 1982.
93. See, for example, *New York Times*, April 7, 1982.
94. *Washington Post*, April 8, 1982.

in the military and in Iran. The combination of tight control by the regime and "Islamizing" the war has created a new institution, the Islamic military.

The Future

The future of the Islamic Iranian military will depend largely on its relationship with the Islamic regime. As a result of its success in the war, the military enjoys a high degree of popularity, but it would be a mistake to expect it to use its renewed status as a springboard back into domestic politics. The regime is well aware of the problems that could arise from such an action and has no intention of allowing the military to gain such influence.

There are several mechanisms by which the regime can control the military and prevent its reentry into politics. One is by giving the military no direct voice in the political arena. In view of Ayatollah Khomeini's admonition to the armed forces not to join political parties,[95] such an action should be fairly easy to carry out. A second is by imbuing the military with a strong revolutionary spirit while preventing it from reverting to a separate class within the society. Some actions have already been taken toward this end, the first of which was the selection of young, aggressive, decidedly Islamic commanders. More significant, however, has been the effort to create a unified Islamic force. Immediately after the victory at Dezful in late March, Tehran announced the formation of a joint military command under the commanders of the regular army and the Revolutionary Guards.[96] This "Pasdarization" (from *Pasdar*, meaning Revolutionary Guard) was one of a series of steps designed to fuse the Guards and the army. Since that time, Guards have commanded some army units and vice versa,[97] but it remains to be seen if the effort to integrate the leadership of the professional military and the Revolutionary Guards will be wholly successful. It is fairly clear, though, that the transformation of the military has created an atmosphere conducive to "Pasdarization."

A third method by which the regime can control the military is reorganization and purge. Throughout the war, especially after the ouster of Bani-Sadr, clandestine radio stations belonging to various Iranian exile groups

95. FBIS, *Daily Report: SAS*, March 16, 1982, p. I2.
96. *Washington Post*, March 30, 1982.
97. Ibid., April 8, 1982.

broadcast periodic announcements of arrests and executions of military officers by the regime.[98] The obvious propaganda intent means that such claims cannot be taken at face value, but because of the pattern established and because names of specific officers were often included, there may be some degree of credibility in the general claim of a continuing purge.[99]

It is quite probable that as soon as the smoke settles over the battle front, possibly even before a peace is achieved, the army will be subjected to another purge. This one, however, will be highly selective. The heroes of this war are not going to be soldiers. The popular mythology will be that the Revolutionary Guards and the popular forces defeated the Iraqi aggressors. To support this half-truth, the regime will have to purge the military of those who became too strong, too popular with the troops, or too effective at leading men in combat, especially if they are not fervent supporters of the regime. Those allowed to remain in the military will be like their commanders, staunchly Islamic. Whatever method of control the regime chooses to use, the result will be a military similar to that envisioned by Mostafa Chamran, a force smaller than the Imperial Military, technically capable, heavily indoctrinated, and carefully watched, but completely under the control of the revolutionary regime.

In spite of the general demobilization that will undoubtedly occur once the war is concluded, the army should remain largely intact. Over the next few years tension along the Iraqi border, along with efforts by recalcitrant tribes in Kurdistan, Baluchistan, and Azerbaijan to gain autonomy, will provide ample reason to keep the army employed. The regime is unlikely to redeploy the military in strength to its old bases near Tehran, preferring to keep it in distant regions. Although the possibility of a coup is remote, the fear of a "colonel on horseback" is pervasive in the regime. Even though the military successfully defended the regime against outside aggressors, it still will not be trusted completely. By keeping most of the army away from Tehran, the regime can be somewhat less concerned about a coup. To be successful in highly centralized Islamic Iran, the perpetrators of a coup would have to have widespread, instantly available public support. Otherwise they would have to seize the mass media and all areas of decisionmaking, all of which are located in Tehran. Without a large body of troops in the immediate vicinity of Tehran, such an action would be extremely difficult.

98. FBIS, *Daily Report: SAS*, October 20, 1981, p. 14; December 1, 1981, p. 111; December 2, 1981, p. 19; and March 17, 1982, p. 112.

99. See, for example, ibid., March 17, 1982, p. 112.

No matter how unpopular the regime may be in the bazaar or among the disenfranchised upper and middle classes, it is supported by the vast lower classes: the peasants and the urban poor. These classes provided most of the volunteers in the Revolutionary Guards, the Army of Twenty Million, and other popular forces that served on the front during the war. Because they are loyal to Ayatollah Khomeini, their support could be somewhat in doubt when he dies, but they, more than other groups in the society, have a stake in the Islamic republic. The seriousness of the economic situation notwithstanding, the lower classes see greater opportunity under the republic than with any other form of government. They are the most devout groups in the society and the most unlikely to turn against the religious leadership. For these reasons, even if a coup was successful, these groups, which have become conditioned to mass protest and revolution, would be unlikely to accept it. Led by the clergy and the seasoned veterans of the war, they would surely oppose the coup in the streets. Unless the coup plotters were willing to incur a bloodbath, the sheer weight of numbers should prevail.

One domestic situation in which the army might conceivably play a role is if some clerical faction called on it for support in a post-Khomeini succession battle. Continued domination of the government by the IRP, supported by the extremely close ties between the IRP and the Revolutionary Guards, make such an event unlikely. It is conceivable, however, that those religious leaders who disagree with Khomeini's doctrine of clerical leadership in government might decide to oppose his successor. In such a situation the military could be a significant factor.